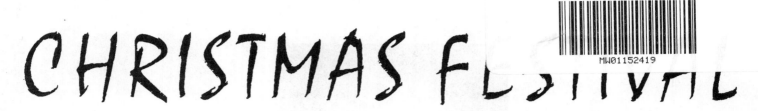

CHRISTMAS FESTIVAL

10 Carol Arrangements for Solo Piano
by
Eugénie Rocherolle

CONTENTS

Editor: JAMES L. KING III
Production Coordinator: KARL BORK
Art Design: JANEL HARRISON

EUGÉNIE ROCHEROLLE

Eugénie Rocherolle, composer, lyricist, pianist, and teacher, began an early publishing career in choral music and in 1978, with the success of her first piano solo collection, established herself as one of the leading American composers of piano repertoire.

A graduate from Newcomb College of Tulane University, Eugénie also had a course of study with Nadia Boulanger in Paris. In 1995 she was honored as the outstanding Newcomb alumna. A "Commissioned by Clavier" composer, she was also one of seven composer members of the National League of American Pen Women whose works were chosen to be presented in a concert at the Terrace Theater in the Kennedy Center. Awards from the Pen Women include a first place for both piano and choral in biennial national competitions. Among her commissions are works for combined chorus and orchestra and for solo and duo piano.

Mrs. Rocherolle's creative output also includes works for solo voice, chorus, concert band, musical theater, and chamber music. Her piano publications include original music for the *WB Solo Library* and the *Composer Spotlight Series,* arrangements for the *WB Christian Piano Library* and *Looney Tunes Piano Library,* as well as independent works for solo piano; one piano, four hands; and two pianos. She is a member of the American Society of Composers, Authors and Publishers (ASCAP); Connecticut Composers Inc.; and the National Federation of Music Clubs. Her biographical profile appears in the *International Who's Who in Music, Baker's Biographical Dictionary of 20th Century Classical Musicians, International Encyclopedia of Women Composers, Who's Who of American Women,* and *Who's Who in the East.*

Mrs. Rocherolle currently maintains a private studio in Connecticut where she teaches piano and composition.

GOD REST YE MERRY, GENTLEMEN

ENGLISH CAROL
Arranged by EUGÉNIE R. ROCHEROLLE

ELM03014

JOY TO THE WORLD
(Sonatina Style)

Music by GEORGE F. HANDEL
Arranged by EUGÉNIE R. ROCHEROLLE

Spirited

O LITTLE TOWN OF BETHLEHEM

LEWIS H. REDNER
Arranged by EUGÉNIE R. ROCHEROLLE

ELM03014

LET IT SNOW! LET IT SNOW! LET IT SNOW!

Words by SAMMY CAHN

Music by JULE STYNE
Arranged by EUGÉNIE R. ROCHEROLLE

8

LULLABY
(Joseph Dear, Oh Joseph Mine)

GERMAN CAROL
Arranged by EUGÉNIE R. ROCHEROLLE

ELM03014

10

ELM03014

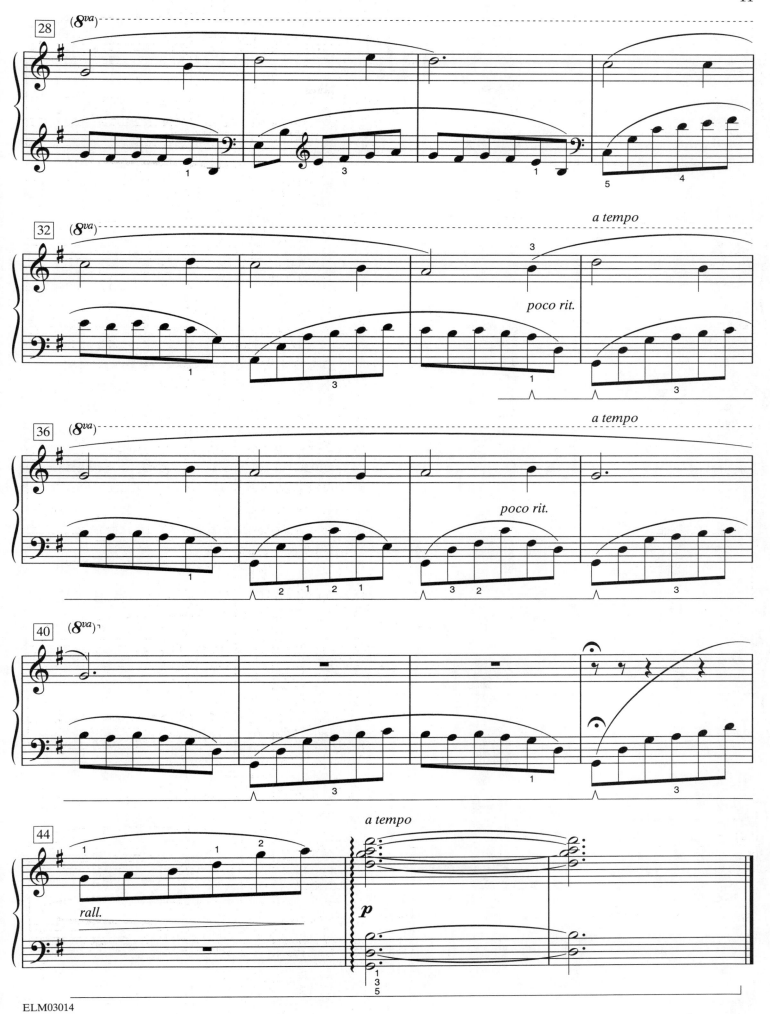

SANTA CLAUS IS COMIN' TO TOWN

Words by HAVEN GILLESPIE

Music by J. FRED COOTS
Arranged by EUGÉNIE R. ROCHEROLLE

ELM03014

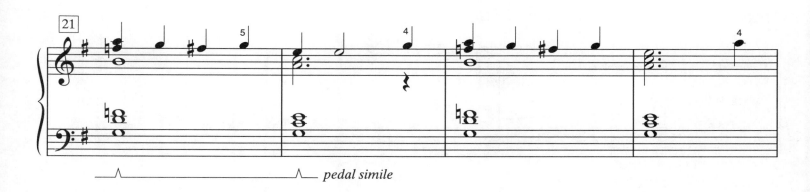

pedal simile

rit.

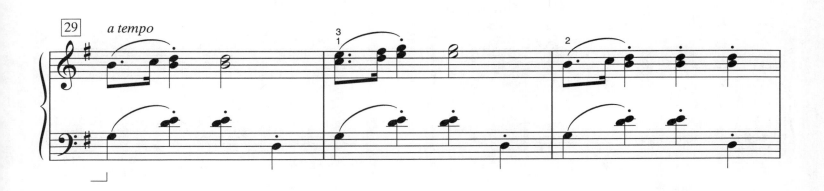

a tempo

ELM03014

14

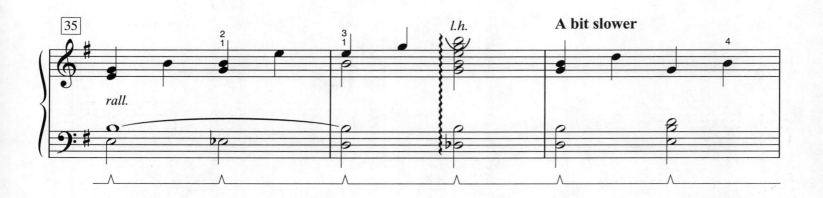

ELM03014

SATIE'S NOEL

OLD ENGLISH CAROL
Arranged by EUGÉNIE R. ROCHEROLLE

ELM03014

16

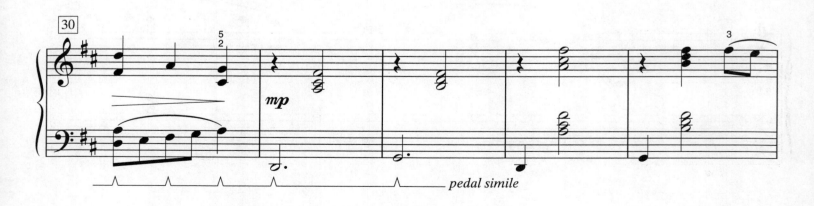

ELM03014

WHAT CHILD IS THIS?

TRADITIONAL ENGLISH MELODY
Arranged by EUGÉNIE R. ROCHEROLLE

WE THREE KINGS

JOHN HENRY HOPKINS
Arranged by EUGÉNIE R. ROCHEROLLE

ELM03014

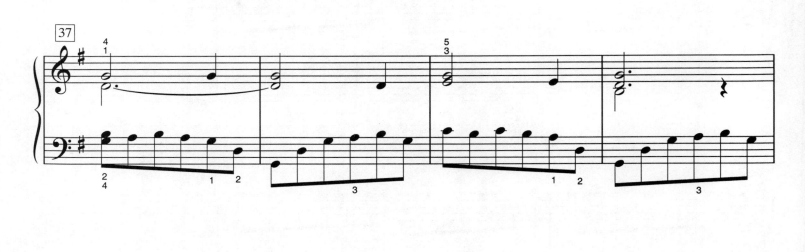

AWAY IN A MANGER
(Cradle Song)

WILLIAM JAMES KIRKPATRICK
Arranged by EUGÉNIE R. ROCHEROLLE

Piano Music
by Eugénie Rocherolle

Piano Solos

Have Yourself a Swingin' Little Christmas
(EL96111)
Each of the seven pieces in this collection receives a unique treatment, with delightful harmonic and rhythmic surprises. You will find a lot of humor, tender dignity ("The Little Drummer Boy"), and a bit of boogie ("All I Want for Christmas") in these pieces.

Impromptu in A-Flat
(PA9513)
The opening tempo is allegro, with a mood change to adagio, returning to a fast tempo before it all fades away. Accessible to late-intermediate students, the solo will also please the most discriminating advanced pianist.

Keyboard Capers
(ELM00024)
This wonderful collection in the *Composer Spotlight Series* features original character pieces for the intermediate pianist. Included are seven pieces: Boogie Train • Dancin' Shoes • Dig It! • Down Home • G-Whiz Blues • Ragamuffin • Summer Blues.

Keyboard Collage
(ELM00022)
Our *Composer Spotlight Series* includes this collection of original works by Eugénie Rocherolle. These intermediate-level pieces offer the student variety and excitement for lessons and recitals. Included are: Big Tease • Dream Waltz • Drifting • Evening Hymn • Memories • Minuet • Saying Goodbye • Wampum Rock.

Master's Medley
(PA9807)
Eugénie Rocherolle said the tunes just followed one after another, fitting together in a seamless solo. In order of appearance are pieces in the style of Bach, Mozart, Beethoven, Schubert, Schumann, Chopin, Brahms, Puccini, Debussy, and Gershwin — a favorite theme of each composer.

Reverie
(PA9514A)
The piece is gentle and peaceful, creating a sense of calm. The left hand flows in harp-like sixteenths with the right hand singing beautifully above. This is Rocherolle in a melodic, reflective mood. It is fine music, a wonderful Debussy-esque experience.

Sonatina No. 1 "Little Classic"
(PA02270)
Written in traditional three-movement form, Sonatina No. 1 definitely does not sound traditional. The unexpected harmonies and mixed meters ensure instant placement as music of today. Rocherolle has provided lyrical right-hand passages that lift this sonatina into the sure-to-be-a-favorite category.

Theme and Variations
(PA02289)
The theme is happy and bright, with a quick tempo. The variations involve harmonic changes, meter changes, and tempo changes, all combined to create a flavor-filled piece.

Three Mazurkas
(PA02425)
Each mazurka (key G, F, A) is an independent work, and each has a distinctive flavor in romantic style.

Three Waltzes
(PA02381)
Rocherolle provides a delightful musical trip for pianists! Titles are: Un Giorno a Roma (A Day in Rome) • Souvenirs de Paris (Memories of Paris) • Brisas del Caribe (Breezes of the Caribbean). They may be performed separately or as a suite.

'Tis the Season
(EL9921)
Stylistically varied, these solos reflect Rocherolle's warm and innovative style. Titles are: Winter Wonderland • The Christmas Waltz • When Blossoms Flowered 'Mid the Snows • It's the Most Wonderful Time of the Year • Christmas Time Is Here • The Twelve Days of Christmas.

Touch of Blue
(ELM00023)
This is a collection filled with the rhythmic diversity and colorful harmonic treatments that have made Eugénie's music famous around the globe. Titles are: Easy Street • Late Train • Lonely Nights • Remembering You • Thinking Blue • Walkin' Home.

A Touch of Romance
(ELM00050)
Rocherolle's *Three Mazurkas* and *Three Waltzes* provide musical insight into romantic styling with lush harmonies, rhythmic freedom, and pianistic virtuosity.

Un Poco Sonatina
(PA9508)
This is a one-movement sonatina. There's humor and happiness, with a melody that wants to sing and play games.

Piano Duets

Christmas for Two
(ELM00057) (one piano, four hands)
These intermediate-level duets will excite students and add a special touch to holiday season recitals. Titles include: The Twelve Days of Christmas • It Came Upon the Midnight Clear • In the Bleak Midwinter • Go Tell It on the Mountain • Gesù Bambino.

The Way We Danced
(PAM0106) (one piano, four hands)
(PAM0005) (two pianos, four hands)
Piano duo teams will thrill at this new suite of dances composed by Eugénie Rocherolle. The five dances are: Tango for Two • "Classic" Rock • Slow Dancin' • A Winsome Waltz • Jitterbug. These late-intermediate level pieces are easy to put together and will bring cheers from the audience. Dances can be used individually or played as a complete set.

AD0324 08/02